Turning Single-Family Properties into Profit$

The Millionaires 10 Step Guidebook for Real Estate Beginners

Dustin Roberts

Turning Single-Family Properties into Profit$ © 2023

Dustin Roberts LLC

ISBN: 9798864023815

In addition positive reviews from wonderful customers like you help other real estate entrepreneurs feel confident about the Turning Single-Family Properties into Profit$ book. Sharing your happy experience will be greatly appreciated!

I hope you enjoy the Turning Single-Family Properties into Profit$ book.

Preface

As a young boy in the vibrant era of the 1980's, I found myself drawn to the hustle and bustle of the real estate world. I was always intrigued by my grandfather's keen eye for opportunities, my father's meticulous work and the natural ease with which numerous family members navigated the labyrinth of real estate. It was as if they spoke a different language, a language of bricks and mortar, blueprints, and property values. I was mesmerized by this world, and I yearned to be a part of it.

In my journey to become a successful entrepreneur, specifically in the realm of single-family properties, I didn't just rely on my passive observations. I actively sought out mentors, those who had painted their success stories across the canvas of real estate. I felt a deep desire to learn from them, to drink in their knowledge, to understand the secrets behind their art of investing.

Now, I'm certainly not professing to be a financial advisor, nor am I promising a golden goose. This book isn't about guarantees or foolproof methods. Instead, it's a narrative of my journey, a tale of my successes, and the wisdom I gleaned from my experiences. The purpose of this book is to share what I've learned in the hope that it will aid you in your journey.

Before you delve further into the pages of this book, I strongly urge you to consult your own financial advisor. Each real estate endeavor has its own unique set of complexities, and it's important to gain multiple perspectives.

I want to share my experiences with you, not as an instructor lecturing you from a pedestal, but as a fellow traveler who has traversed the path you are about to embark upon. There's much to learn from the successes and the missteps, the triumphs and the hurdles. My hope is that my journey will inspire and guide you on yours.

I invite you to join me on this journey, a journey where learning is an adventure, where each page turn reveals a new insight, a new nugget of wisdom.

Remember, the world of real estate isn't just about property and profits, it's about people and their dreams. It's about building homes, not just houses. It's about making wise investments, not just monetary transactions.

Dustin Roberts

4

Table of Contents

Step 1: Why Real Estate Investing?

Have you ever asked, "Why should I invest in single-family properties?" Trust me, I've been there, asking myself the same question at the dawn of my career. The journey of real estate investing is indeed thrilling, full of rewards, but it requires a deep understanding of why you're embarking on it in the first place.

Your why is your anchor, the bedrock upon which you'll construct your real estate empire. It's the force that pushes you forward when challenges arise. It's why you'll stand up again, even when you stumble.

The 'why' could be unique for everyone. For some, it may be to attain financial freedom, while others might be inspired by the prospect of wealth accumulation or ensuring a secure retirement. You can tread new career paths, escape the constant hustle and bustle, or gain the freedom to spend time on what truly matters to you. **The first step on this journey is to unearth your 'why.'**

Once your 'why' anchor is firmly set, it's time to chart out the course - to convert your 'why' into measurable, specific goals. Let's say your 'why' is financial independence. You need to translate this broad target into concise goals, such as generating a particular monthly rental income. It could also be attaining a certain profit level from property sales within a specific time frame. Having tangible, well-laid-out goals can act as your compass, guiding your steps and helping you gauge your progress.

My Personal Voyage: Escaping the Rat Race

I remember vividly the early days of my real estate journey. My 'why' was escaping the constraints of the rat race and dedicating more time to my loved ones. I set out with a simple goal: to acquire a property that would generate sufficient income, not just to cover all monthly expenses, but to bring about a positive cash flow.

Let's say the total of your tenant's monthly rent surpasses the sum of your property's mortgage, tax, insurance, and maintenance. The excess is what I call a 'positive cash flow.' Robert Kiyosaki, a well-known real estate investor, once posed two thought-provoking questions:

1. *How many properties can you afford that lose a few hundred dollars monthly?*
2. *How many properties can you afford that yield a positive cash flow of a few hundred dollars monthly?*

To me, the answers were clear. I couldn't afford many properties that bled money, but I could accumulate as many properties as possible that generated a positive cash flow. I followed this path with unwavering determination because a consistent positive cash flow would bring me closer to escaping the rat race.

The Essence: Positive Cash Flow

The cornerstone of my strategy was focusing on positive cash flow. This approach, while simple, was the key that unlocked my journey towards financial independence. And it's a journey that I believe anyone, including you, can embark on.

In embarking on your real estate journey, remember the importance of understanding your 'why,' setting clear goals, and focusing on positive cash flow properties. This journey might not always be smooth, but I promise it will be worth it. As we progress through this book, I hope to guide you through the complexities and nuances of real estate investing, making the journey not just rewarding, but also enjoyable.

Step 2: The Blueprint of Building Your Real Estate Dream Team

Let me let you in on a little secret. The journey to success in real estate investing, specifically with single-family properties, isn't a solo expedition. It's a thrilling adventure, navigated with an ensemble cast of professionals.

Reflecting on my humble beginnings in the realm of real estate investing, it's clear to me how pivotal my team was in my ascent to success. Picture, if you will, a group of individuals, each with unique expertise and experience, congregating to aid you in your journey towards real estate investment triumph.

So, who's in this group? Well, from lenders to contractors, realtors to title attorneys, bankers, public accountants, and insurers, the list goes on. Imagine sitting at a round table with these experts, each bringing their invaluable insights, ensuring that every decision you make is informed and every risk is mitigated. Trust me, the confidence this collective knowledge inspires is priceless.

The Lender: Your Financial Backstop

Let's take a moment to talk about lenders, the unsung heroes of your real estate investment journey. You might have an eye for the perfect property, but without the necessary funding, that dream house remains just that, a dream. Lenders help you make the dream a reality.

They provide mortgages, private loans, and an array of other financing solutions, consistently ensuring that you have the capital you need to add properties to your portfolio. I've personally funded my properties through credit cards, HELOC (Home Equity Line of Credit), and even investor-friendly community banks. Though I haven't used them myself, I've known investors who've creatively utilized hard money lenders and self-directed Roth IRAs for real estate.

Let me paint a picture of my first investment venture. I had my eyes on a quaint single-family home with a purchase price of $100,000. A local bank loaned me $80,000, and I used a HELOC from my personal residence to cover the remaining $20,000. The result? A successfully financed investment property, and a major milestone in my real estate journey.

The financing process can seem overwhelming, especially for the uninitiated. Therefore, I **strongly recommend** that you consult with a financial advisor before you dive in. Remember, knowledge is power, and a little bit of guidance can go a long way.

The Contractors: More than Just Hammers and Nails

The role of a contractor extends far beyond simple hammer-and-nail tasks. They are project overseers, budget controllers, team coordinators, and quality guarantors. They ensure every project aligns perfectly with your vision, while also sticking to the building codes and schedules.

Contractors can specialize in a range of areas such as electrical, plumbing, carpentry, masonry, iron or steel work, painting, roofing, HVAC or landscaping, and more. Think of them as the multi-talented artists of the real estate world, capable of creating masterpieces in their respective fields.

Now, you might wonder, "Where do I find these incredible professionals?" Well, the search for contractors can be as exciting as a treasure hunt. You can embark on this adventure through several routes:

1. **Online Directories and Associations:** Websites like the Associated Builders and Contractors can be a good starting point. They have listings of contracting companies, making it easier for you to shortlist potential candidates.

2. **Referrals:** Nothing beats a good old referral. Ask your network of professionals for their recommendations. The chances are that someone in your circle might know a reputable contractor who can do wonders for your property.

3. **Search Engine Business Listings and Social Media:** The digital world has made everything accessible at our fingertips. You can check out business listings on search engines and social media platforms. This way, you also get to read reviews of a contractor's work, helping you make an informed decision.

I vividly remember the process I followed to choose the contractor for my first single-family investment property. I had understood the type of contractor I needed, and I interviewed at least three of them to gauge their work style and expertise. I also made sure to follow up on referrals provided by the contractors.

Eventually, I found my perfect match in a contractor from my town's local real estate investors association (REIA). It was like finding the missing piece of a puzzle. He brought my vision to life, transforming the property into a beautiful and inviting space.

Realtors: The Custodians of Your Property Dreams

Trust me when I say this – a great realtor is worth their weight in gold. They are the ones who translate your investment dreams into reality. And not just any reality, but the kind that results in a steady flow of income and builds your wealth in the long run.

From my experience, the relationship with my realtor has been just as important as the properties themselves. Picture a realtor as a beacon, guiding you through the complexity of the real estate market, illuminating the path to your dream single-family properties. They have a unique access key to the treasure trove known as the Multiple Listing Service (MLS), and can help you unearth potential gems in the property market.

I vividly remember my first interaction with a realtor. I had just started out in the world of real estate investing. I was filled with enthusiasm, fueled by the desire to make wise investments, but I was also nervous - for the real estate world was unknown to me. In came my realtor, a referral from a close friend. She specialized in foreclosed single-family properties, and her manner was inviting and warm, her expertise evident. With her guidance, I was able to purchase my first few investment properties at a steal. These properties turned out to be great investments, thanks to their lucrative locations and potential for value appreciation. It was a major milestone in my real estate journey.

How do you find such a guide? Here are a few steps to take:

1. **Referrals:** Ask people you trust. Friends, family, and colleagues can be a great resource. They can share their experiences and might even introduce you to a stellar realtor.

2. **Professional Associations:** Look into local real estate investors associations (REIAs). These groups often have dedicated realtors who are familiar with the needs of investors.

3. **Interviews:** Don't be afraid to ask questions. I always interviewed at least three realtors before deciding to work with one. Some questions that helped me were: How long have you been a realtor? Do you have experience working with investors? Can you share your experience with helping other first-time real estate investors?

Remember, choosing a realtor is not a decision you make on a whim. It's a choice that can shape your investment journey. A good realtor can open doors to opportunities you never knew existed.

A competent realtor is your ally in buying and selling. But they're also so much more. They're your negotiator, your market analyst, and your advocate. They understand the pulse of the real estate market, and they can give you valuable insights into trends that could impact your investment decisions.

While I can preach about the importance of a realtor, it's important to remember that the choice is ultimately yours.

Title Attorney: The Legal Torchbearer

Picture this: you've found your dream single-family property, the perfect addition to your investment portfolio. But halt! There's a roadblock. A question that demands your attention - is the property's title clear and free of any liens or disputes? This is the juncture in your journey where you'll need a title attorney, your legal torchbearer.

A title attorney is like a guardian of your investment journey. They ensure that the single-family property you're eyeing has a clear title - in other words, the title is free from any legal conflicts or disputes that could become your nightmare in the future. They handle the legal aspects of the transaction, which includes conducting title searches, drafting documentation, and presiding over the closing procedures.

Always remember this: *a successful real estate transaction requires a thoroughly scrutinized title of the subject property.* When acquiring a single-family property, one of the most important prerequisites I have for a seller of the subject property is a clear title.

What does it mean when we talk about a 'clear' title? In general, we are looking for a title to be marketable and insurable at the time of a real estate closing. A *marketable* title means it is clear, free from legal flaws, and in good standing. It is something a reasonable buyer would accept without hesitation, confident in its legality and legitimacy.

The second pillar, *insurable,* refers to a title that can be insured by a title insurance company. This insurance provides a safety net, protecting the policyholder against financial loss that might arise from defects in the title. It's like having a sturdy umbrella that shields you from unforeseen storms!

Reflecting on my own journey, I've interacted with multiple title attorneys in the past. Over time, I realized that when you use the same title attorney or title company whenever possible, the transaction process becomes smooth like a well-oiled machine. This familiarity breeds trust and efficiency, essential ingredients for a successful real estate transaction.

When I was stepping onto the path of real estate investments for the very first time, I used a title company recommended by my lender for my first single-family investment property. Their expertise and professionalism made the process seamless, and I've been a repeat customer of a few investor-friendly title companies ever since. These companies have shown a high degree of flexibility and adaptability with deal structures involving business entities like a trust or a limited liability corporation (LLC).

The question now is: how do you find such a reliable title attorney or company? The answer lies in diligent research and leveraging your professional network. I found success in using referrals from lenders, realtors, and other real estate investors. You'd be surprised at the extent and richness of the collective knowledge in your professional circle!

Additionally, I've also benefited from reviews available on search engines and social media platforms. These platforms offer a plethora of information from real users, helping you make an informed decision - a decision that could make or break your investment journey.

Your Banker: The Financial Architect

Just like a good story needs a compelling protagonist, your real estate investment journey needs a trusted partner. That role is often helmed by a banker, your financial architect.

Bankers aren't just about numbers and spreadsheets. They are about building relationships, understanding your financial aspirations, and helping you navigate the financial decisions. I've always appreciated the personal connection I've established with my bankers. They've been my financial sounding board, always ready to offer advice, brainstorm solutions, and simplify the complexities of real estate investing.

In my experience, smaller local banks can offer a user-friendly experience compared to their larger counterparts. Why, you might ask? The answer lies in personal attention. Local banks are more in tune with the community's needs and offer a tailored approach that can make all the difference to your investment experience. Using a smaller bank for my first single-family investment property was one of the best decisions I made. I felt heard, valued, and, most importantly, supported.

A good banker plays an integral role in managing your investment finances. They help you set up accounts for rental income, handle mortgage payments, and provide financial advice related to your property. This becomes particularly important when you're juggling multiple investments. I remember the sense of calm I felt when setting up my first rental income account. It was like I had a personal assistant, neatly organizing my finances and freeing me up to focus on my next investment.

If you're investing through a trut, a LLC or another entity, your banker can also assist with business banking services. I've utilized this service for several property investments and found it invaluable. It has provided me with flexibility, control, and a streamlined view of my investment portfolio.

The Public Accountant: Your Financial Navigator

These people of numbers specialize in tax planning and accounting, serving as your in-house financial analyst. They essentially decode the complex matrix of tax regulations and translate it into a language we can all understand - the language of potential savings and increased profits. A good public accountant isn't just a number-cruncher, but a key player in your real estate investing team.

When it comes to your single-family investment properties, having a public accountant on your team can be likened to having a seasoned coach guiding a football squad. Their primary role is to help structure your real estate investments for maximum tax efficiency.

Imagine this - you've just closed a lucrative deal and are basking in the success of your new acquisition. But then, tax season rolls around, and you find yourself in a maze of forms, calculations, and potential miscalculations. I've been there, and trust me, it's not a fun place to be. That's where your public accountant comes into play. They handle tax preparations, ensuring that your returns adhere to the ever-changing tax regulations.

Having an eagle-eyed view of your financial portfolio is critical in real estate investing. A public accountant helps you do just that. They provide a 360-degree view of your investments, identifying trends, and spotting opportunities for growth. Their analytical skills can pinpoint patterns that you might miss, offering you invaluable insights to optimize your portfolio.

One of the most powerful tools in a real estate investor's kit is the 1031 exchange. Simply put, a 1031 exchange allows investors to defer paying capital gains taxes when they sell a property and reinvest the proceeds in a similar property. If used wisely, 1031 exchanges can potentially save you a fortune in taxes, helping you grow your wealth exponentially.

Insurer: Your Safety Net

They cushion you against the unpredictable, the unforeseen circumstances that could otherwise send your investment portfolio into a tailspin. Their role is to help you secure the necessary insurance coverage for your single-family properties, ensuring you're covered against all possible risks.

At a minimum, you need to understand three types of policies:

1. *Landlord policy for your rented property*
2. *Vacant dwelling policy for a property you're renovating*
3. *Builder's Risk for your property undergoing a major renovation*

These policies ensure that you're not left high and dry if a tenant damages your property, a storm hits during renovation, or a major construction mishap occurs.

The ultimate strategy, however, is liability coverage. This is your overarching shield, protecting your investments and mitigating risks. Real estate investing is fraught with unforeseen circumstances. Natural disasters, disgruntled tenants, unexpected renovation costs - the list goes on. This is where your insurer comes in, offering a layer of protection that allows you to sleep peacefully at night.

When it comes to selecting an insurance professional, it's important to understand the difference between an insurance agent and an insurance broker. An insurance agent often represents only one carrier, such as Allstate or Liberty Mutual. On the other hand, an insurance broker can represent several insurance companies.

This difference might seem trivial, but it has significant implications.

The advantage of working with a broker is that they have the flexibility to creatively insure a difficult property. They have access to multiple carriers, which means they can compare options and find the best fit for your needs. Personally, as I acquired my third property, I found it most strategic and cost-effective to switch to an experienced insurance broker.

If you're wondering how to find a reliable insurer, here's a little anecdote from my journey. The insurance broker that I still use today was referred to me by one of my first real estate mentors. Just as in other aspects of the investing journey, networking and mentorship were key.

I've also reinforced my understanding of policies through self-education. It's vitally important to understand your existing policies on your properties and have a seasoned insurance broker as part of your real estate investing team.

Tapping into the Power of Local Real Estate Investors Associations

Have you ever wondered where the wealth of knowledge lies in real estate investing? The answer is within the local Real Estate Investors Associations (REIAs). These associations have proven to be the golden key in my own journey, unlocking access to an invaluable network of seasoned investors, trusted professionals, and resources tailored to the dynamics of our local real estate market.

In the early stages of my career, as I was just beginning to dip my toes into the vast ocean of real estate investing, I stumbled upon my local REIA. Simply put, it was like finding a treasure trove. I discovered that these associations weren't just groups of like-minded individuals, but a powerful gathering of knowledge, insights, and firsthand experiences.

Looking back now, joining my local REIA wasn't just a strategic move; it was the game-changer. The connections I made there, the wisdom I gathered, and the relationships I built have not only accelerated my investing journey but also enriched it in ways I hadn't imagined at the outset.

As you can tell by now I'm certainly an advocate for joining a local REIA. They're not just about networking opportunities, although that is definitely a crucial aspect. Your local REIA is about education and the power of collective wisdom. It's about tapping into a community of fellow investors who have walked the path you're embarking on and learning from their successes and stumbles.

REIAs often host seminars, workshops, and interactive sessions that serve as a platform for learning and growth. My first workshop on single-family property investing was a real eye-opener, revealing the intricacies of the market and offering practical strategies and solutions.

They also provide access to resources that are specifically designed for the local real estate dynamics. These range from market trends and investment opportunities to legal regulations and financial considerations. It's like having a curated guidebook at your fingertips, one that's continuously updated to reflect the ever-changing landscape of real estate.

Another factor that makes REIAs so valuable is their list of trusted professionals who are well-versed in local real estate. The professionals recommended by REIAs understand the unique challenges and opportunities in your area and have proven their reliability and efficiency to fellow investors.

What I appreciate most about my REIA experience is the lasting relationships I've built. Be it my mentor who guided me through my initial hiccups, fellow investors who've shared their insights and experiences, or professionals who've assisted me in various transactions, the people I've met through REIAs have left an indelible mark on my journey.

Close-knit, supportive, and grounded, my local REIA feels like a family. A family that's always ready to lend a hand, share advice, and celebrate each other's success. It's this sense of community, camaraderie, and shared purpose that makes REIAs a truly unique and valuable resource for any aspiring real estate investor.

Building a Cohesive and High-Performing Real Estate Team: A Step-by-Step Guide

Your team is as much a part of your investment portfolio as the properties you invest in. But how do you go about assembling this dream team? And once you've assembled it, how do you ensure it functions like a well-oiled machine? Let's dive in.

The Art of Interviewing: Selecting the Right People for Your Team

First things first, selecting the right individuals to be part of your team is absolutely crucial. This isn't about collecting as many professionals as you can, it's about finding the right individuals whose skills, experience, and vision align with yours. *Remember, quality over quantity.*

When interviewing potential team members, make sure to look beyond their qualifications and experience. Yes, their track record is important, but what's equally important is their approach towards real estate investing. Is it in line with your own views? Do they share similar values and ethics? These can be pivotal in shaping your relationship down the line.

Effective Team Management: Nurturing a High-Performing Team

Once you've built your team, the next big question is - how do you ensure they function effectively? The key here is clear communication, setting expectations right at the outset, and regularly assessing performance.

Another crucial aspect of team management is defining roles and responsibilities. Each member of your team should know exactly what their role is and what's expected of them.

For instance, when I brought on a local banker, we sat down and outlined his role in detail – setting up accounts, managing mortgage payments, providing financial advice, and so on. This clarity not only helped him understand his responsibilities but also allowed us to work seamlessly together.

Dealing with Challenges: Making Tough Decisions

Now, here comes the hard part. There will be times when you'll need to make tough decisions. Maybe a team member isn't living up to your expectations. Maybe your investment strategy has evolved and your team needs to evolve with it. In such cases, don't hesitate to make changes. After all, your team is an extension of your investment strategy, and if it's not providing the required support, changes are necessary.

In conclusion, remember that building and managing a high-performing real estate team is an ongoing process. There's no 'one size fits all' approach. It's about continuously evaluating and adjusting your team to meet your evolving needs. It's about ensuring that your team isn't just a group of professionals, but a cohesive unit that's working towards a common goal. Because, in the end, that's what truly fuels success in the world of real estate investing.

Step 3: Know Your Local Area

The pulse of your local area is crucial to your investments. You see, it's like knowing where the best apples grow in an orchard, as **knowledge is the compass of investing**. Start by becoming a detective in your local area. Dive deep into the quality of local schools, the major employers setting the economic pace, the local attractions magnetizing visitors, and the average cost, size, and features of single-family properties in your area.

Understanding Neighborhoods

As an experienced real estate investor, I can tell you that one of the most fascinating and rewarding parts of this business is the journey of **discovering the uniqueness of every neighborhood**. Just like people, each neighborhood carries its own character, stories, and nuances. Every corner tells a story, and understanding that narrative is what makes you a great investor.

Ever heard the phrase **"location, location, location"**? I bet you have! It's one of the most common pieces of advice given to new investors. But what does it really mean? It means that the fortunes of a property are intrinsically tied to the area it is set in. Neighborhoods aren't just about streets and houses; they are about the communities, the schools, the economy, and the aura. All of this comes together to form the 'location' factor.

Now, when I talk about understanding a neighborhood, the first thing that comes to mind is safety. As a proud father myself, I know the importance of a **safe and secure environment** for families. I've seen some neighborhoods transform from challenging areas to family friendly environments, all because investors like us cared about the safety of our communities. Believe me, trying neighborhoods are more than just challenges; they tell a story of the neighborhood's past, present, and future.

Would you prefer to live in a place with easy access to shopping, entertainment, and parks, or a place that's isolated from everything? I bet your answer is the former! **Proximity to amenities** can significantly impact the desirability of properties and the overall investment potential. People love convenience, and as an investor, meeting this need can be a game-changer.

I often tell my mentees, "investing in real estate is like planting a seed and watching it grow." The growth of a neighborhood is reflected in its **property appreciation history**. A neighborhood that has consistently demonstrated property value growth over the years is usually a safe bet for your investment.

Finally, the end goal of understanding neighborhoods is to determine their overall desirability. Because let's face it, the ultimate test of a property's value is how much someone desires to live there. **Neighborhood desirability** can be a subjective field, and there's no one-size-fits-all strategy here. So, use your understanding of the factors we've discussed so far, blend it with your intuition, and make an informed decision.

Evaluating Local Schools - The Unseen Goldmine

I genuinely believe education and real estate go hand in hand. Yes, you heard it right. Schools aren't just about books and benches, they're also a significant driver of property value. Let me share a bit more about this.

Let's take a step back and think about our own lives for a moment. Can you remember the time when you were looking for your first home or when you considered moving to a more desirable neighborhood? What were the things that mattered the most to you? Convenience, amenities, and safety, of course, but what about schools? For most of us with families, the **quality of local schools** is a top priority. It's a factor that can greatly impact our decision when choosing a place to live.

Schools are an invisible goldmine when it comes to real estate investments. Properties in areas with highly-rated schools command higher rents and are likely to appreciate better in the long run.

Now, let's talk about how to evaluate these potential goldmines. You'll need to do your homework here. Start by researching information about the local school districts. Look for their rankings, check the availability of educational facilities, and if possible, get a feel of the general sentiment about these schools in the community. This can tremendously **enhance your property's appeal and rental potential**.

I've observed that neighborhoods with great schools tend to attract a stable, family-oriented populace. These families are more likely to put down roots and stay for longer periods. This means **consistent rental revenue** and a higher chance of property value appreciation for you.

So, don't just take this as a passing note. Make this your mantra. **Great Schools = Great Investments.**

Understanding the Power of Employment Opportunities

Now, let's change gears a bit and move our focus to another crucial component that often gets pushed to the background - **Employment Opportunities**. Honestly, I cannot emphasize enough on the importance of this factor.

Consider the job market as the backbone of a region. When it's strong, it holds everything together. It's that simple! The local job market plays a vital role in your real estate investment journey. Areas with a robust and diversified economy tend to maintain more stable property markets. But how do you assess that?

Dive deep into the primary industries that drive the local economy. Are they thriving or struggling? The health of these industries can have a substantial impact on the property value. Next, look at the job growth trends in your area. Has there been an upward trajectory? Or is it stagnant, or worse, declining? A growing job market indicates economic stability, which, in turn, makes the area more attractive to tenants and potential buyers.

Remember, when people have stable jobs, they have consistent income. And when they have consistent income, they make reliable tenants. This makes areas with thriving job opportunities a magnet for potential renters.

Now, let's talk about the employers. Who are the major players shaping the local economy? Are they stable, or are there rumors of layoffs and downsizing? A strong employer landscape means more potential renters, and that's music to an investor's ears!

A robust job market doesn't just bring in potential renters. It also triggers a ripple effect. More jobs mean more people, which leads to increased demand for goods and services. This growth can fuel the development of new amenities, making the area even more desirable from a real estate investment perspective.

Lastly, I want to talk about something I consider the holy grail of a strong job market - diversification. An area that relies on a single industry is vulnerable. But an area with a diversified job market is resilient, and resilience is key to long-term investment success.

Exploring Local Attractions

When we think about real estate, our mind often gravitates toward figures, profits, and the technical aspects of property investment. However, there's a more human side to it that we often overlook.

Think about it. Your property doesn't sit in isolation. It's a part of a larger community, a neighborhood that's teeming with life and experiences. It's nestled in an environment that's vibrant, brimming with a life of its own. The local attractions around your property play a significant role in shaping these experiences.

Consider parks and green spaces, for instance. A property close to a park means a world of opportunities. It means weekend picnics under the shade of a tree, it means children playing in the open, it means a chance for families to escape the urban rush and soak in nature's beauty. It's not just about aesthetics or recreation. The proximity to parks and green spaces can impact the physical and mental wellbeing of the residents.

And what about shopping centers? At first glance, they're merely places for retail therapy. But dig a little deeper, and you'll find they're more than that. They're modern-day community centers, places where people meet, bond, and create shared experiences. Living close to a shopping center adds a layer of convenience and social engagement to the lives of the people.

Entertainment venues, on the other hand, speak volumes about the cultural pulse of a neighborhood. They reflect the local identity and character, be it a theater showcasing local talent or a music venue pulsating with the rhythm of the community. These venues can be a big draw for people seeking a culturally rich living environment.

Lastly, public transportation. In today's urban environments, efficient public transportation isn't just a luxury; it's a necessity. A property with easy access to public transportation can significantly enhance the quality of life for the residents, saving them time and resources on daily commutes.

Each of these elements contributes to the bigger picture of 'place'. Remember, as investors in single-family properties, we're not just investing in bricks and mortar. We're investing in homes, in places where people shape their lives, where they create memories. And the richness of these experiences is often tied to the local attractions around them.

Analyzing Property Values

Analyzing property values may initially seem like a complicated maze of numbers and trends. But let's break it down to its core essence. At its heart, analyzing property value is about understanding the historical ebb and flow of property prices in your chosen area. It's about learning from the past to anticipate the future.

This information is the bedrock for making prudent decisions about property acquisition, setting competitive pricing, and forecasting your potential return on investment. But that's not all - this data can also affect your property tax liability. You see, the higher the value of your property, the higher your property tax.

Property values are not static. They are dynamic, constantly fluctuating based on a host of factors. On one end of the spectrum, we have appreciation. This is when the value of a property increases over time. On the flip side, there's depreciation - a decline in the value of a property.

Being able to distinguish between these two trends is crucial in the world of real estate investing. It could be the difference between a sound investment and a financial sinkhole.

If a neighborhood has a history of steady appreciation, it's a solid indication that your property's value may continue to grow in the future. However, if the past data shows a downward trend, it may be a red flag, indicating that your investment might not yield the desired returns.

Let's take this a step further. Looking at historical data isn't just about identifying trends. It's about understanding why these

27

trends occurred. Was there a rise in employment opportunities? Was there a new school district that attracted families to the area, thus increasing the demand for housing? Or was there an economic downturn that affected the local job market and led to a dip in property values?

Now let's discuss the 'how'. How exactly do you analyze these property values? The process isn't as intimidating as it might seem.

Start by collecting historical data on property prices in your area. This data is often available through local government agencies or online real estate portals. Next, delve into the data. Look out for patterns and trends. Was there a year when property prices spiked? Or was there a period of decline? Then, try to understand what caused these fluctuations. This part of the process may require a bit of detective work. Look at the economic trends during that time. Was there an industry boom or an economic recession? Were there changes in the local community that could have influenced property prices?

Here's a tale from the trenches of real estate that really stands out - I once flipped a single-family home, the proverbial ugly duckling in a neighborhood brimming with potential. When I first laid eyes on it, I estimated its post-renovation value would hover around the $350,000 mark, a figure backed by an exhaustive analysis of similar properties in the area. But as the makeover unfolded, so too did the neighborhood's demographic landscape. An unexpected surge of newcomers flooded the local real estate market, creating a ripple effect that sent property values skyrocketing. To my surprise, this trailblazer of a home ended up selling for a staggering $450,000. That's a full $100,000 over my initial estimate! Talk about a thrilling twist in the plot.

Lastly, use this information to make educated predictions about future trends. This final step ties back to the essence of property value analysis – using the past to anticipate the future.

Knowing Typical Property Characteristics

The Average Size Matters

Size, here, does not merely refer to the physical dimensions of the property. It's about understanding the space that a typical local family would require. This could range from small, cozy homes to larger properties with ample room for growth. Knowing this information can help you gauge the scope and scale of your potential investment.

I've observed that areas with larger average property sizes often attract families looking for space and comfort. Conversely, regions with smaller properties appeal to young professionals or couples starting their life journey. The key is to understand your target market and find properties that cater to their needs.

Number of Bedrooms and Bathrooms: More Than Just Numbers

The number of bedrooms and bathrooms in a property may seem like a mere statistic at first glance. However, these numbers tell a story - a story about the potential lifestyle of the residents.

As one would expect, a property with multiple bedrooms might draw larger families, while properties with fewer bedrooms attract young professionals or couples. The number of bathrooms, too, is a significant factor. Multiple bathrooms suggest convenience and privacy, and this could be a significant draw for families with older children.

Let me share a couple of transformative experiences about rental properties I ventured into many years ago. One of my remarkable transformations was repurposing a garage into a functional living space, drastically increasing the potential of the property. Imagine a cozy 3-bedroom, 2-bathroom house evolving into a spacious 4-bedroom, 2-bathroom single-family haven, all thanks to an enclosed garage. This smart renovation not only increased the square footage but also significantly elevated the monthly rental income.

In a similar vein, another property was given a fresh lease on life when we converted the carport into a bedroom and a bathroom. What was once a humble 3-bedroom, 1-bathroom abode emerged as a comfortable 4-bedroom, 2-bathroom single-family home. The newfound space, combined with the added amenities, led to an appreciable surge in the monthly lease figures. These experiences underscore the amazing potential concealed within spaces often overlooked.

From an investor's perspective, understanding these nuances can help you make informed decisions about which properties to invest in. It will also help you tailor your property to meet local expectations, giving you an edge in a competitive market.

Common Features: The Icing on the Cake

Once you've understood the core characteristics - size, bedrooms, and bathrooms - it's time to look at the 'icing on the cake'. The common features found in local properties.

Is there a trend towards open floor plans or gourmet kitchens? Do properties in the area often come with large yards or home offices? These features can significantly enhance a property's appeal to potential renters or buyers, and knowing what's popular in your area can help you make impactful renovations or additions.

Beyond the Statistics

I want you to remember - numbers and statistics are just the tip of the iceberg. They provide a baseline for understanding the typical property characteristics, but the true magic lies in interpreting these numbers, and in understanding the stories they tell.

The average size, the number of bedrooms and bathrooms, the common features - these characteristics are not just statistics to be glanced over. They are snippets of the potential lifestyle a property can offer to its residents.

Understanding these characteristics is like holding a map in your journey of real estate investing. It's about knowing the landscape, identifying the most promising paths, and making informed decisions that align with your investment goals and the needs of your target market.

Understand the characteristics, understand the community, and pave your way to successful real estate investing in single-family properties.

Step 4: Begin with the End in Mind

Imagine the Future, Today. The fascinating thing about real estate investing is that it's not a one-size-fits-all kind of deal. There are multiple strategies you can employ, each with its unique approach and mindset.

For instance, you could opt to wholesale your property to another buyer, a quick and cash-efficient method. On the other hand, you might choose to renovate and resell, a strategy that often requires patience and predilection for managing renovation projects.

Alternatively, you might renovate and then rent it out, a long-term investment that offers steady income and potential appreciation. Each strategy is as unique as you are, and understanding what suits you best is critical.

The clearer your vision is, the more informed your decisions will be throughout the investment process. Think about it, would you start a journey without knowing your destination? Probably not. It's the same with investing in single-family properties. You need to know where you're headed so you can plan your route accordingly.

The Business Plan

A solid business plan outlines your objectives and chosen strategy. It's your own personal field guide to investing. Whether you plan to wholesale, renovate and resell, or renovate and rent, your business plan ensures you're prepared for the journey ahead.

It doesn't stop there. A robust business plan goes a step further, detailing your financing plan, property criteria and projected timelines. It even includes financial projections, a risk assessment, and an exit strategy for each investment.

This might sound like a lot, but trust me, once you get started, it becomes second nature. It's as simple as riding a bike—once you learn how, you never forget.

A well-crafted business plan does three key things:

1. *It gives you **clarity**. It's like having a GPS in your car. You always know where you're going and how to get there.*

2. *It helps secure **financing**. Banks and lenders love to see a clear, well-thought-out plan. It shows them you're serious about your investment.*

3. *It serves as a **progress tracker**. Life is unpredictable and real estate is no different. Having a business plan helps you stay on course, even when you hit unexpected bumps in the road.*

Every investor is unique. You have your own goals, dreams, and circumstances. That's what's so fantastic about real estate investing—the pathways are as diverse as the people who walk them.

As a seasoned investor myself, I've found that there are three common paths that investors often follow:

Wholesaling

Wholesaling, at its core, is all about being a savvy dealmaker. It's about spotting those hidden gems, those undervalued properties, and securing them before anyone else does. But remember, it's not about hoarding these properties for yourself, quite the contrary. You're the middleman, or I prefer to think of it as the *bridge,* linking the property seller with an end investor or end buyer.

Let's break it down a bit. In wholesaling, negotiation is king. It's about knowing your market, having your finger on its pulse, and being able to adjust your approach to suit the situation. The successful wholesaler knows when to play the soft notes and when to hit the high ones.

Now, this wouldn't be a complete discussion about wholesaling without talking about how to spot undervalued properties. There's a certain knack to it, a sixth sense that you develop over time. It's about seeing potential where others just see a rundown property.

But let's not rely on intuition alone. Data is your friend here. Look for signs of a motivated seller—perhaps they've had continuous listings, or they're looking to sell quickly due to a move or financial pressure. These are potential gold mines for a wholesaler.

Finally, let's talk profits. The key to wholesaling lies in the spread—the difference between what you contract the property for and what you sell that contract for. Imagine this scenario—you come across a seller looking to quickly offload a property valued at $350,000. You step in, negotiate, and secure a contract to purchase for $300,000. Then, you turn around and assign the contract to a buyer for $320,000. That $20,000 difference? That's your profit.

Wholesaling isn't for everyone. It requires a certain mindset, a willingness to hustle, and the ability to see potential where others don't. But for those of you who choose this path, it can be a thrilling and profitable journey.

Renovating and Reselling

Let's turn our attention to another strategy, an equally exciting pathway in real estate investment: renovating and reselling, often fondly referred to as **"flipping."**

Picture this: you stumble upon a property that's seen better days, a place that's lost its sparkle. You take that property, breathe new life into it with smart renovations, and then sell it for a premium. That is flipping.

I've always found flipping to be an engaging and rewarding strategy. It's like uncovering a diamond in the rough and polishing it until it shines brilliantly. But, let's be clear here, this strategy isn't for the faint-hearted. It takes grit, it takes a keen eye for detail, and most importantly, it requires a solid understanding of renovation costs and real estate market trends.

Remember this: the crux of flipping lies in **buying at the right price, renovating efficiently,** and **selling at a profit.**

You sell the renovated property at a higher price, and the profit starts rolling in. You've successfully flipped a property. But the reward isn't just in the profit. There's a distinct sense of satisfaction in seeing a property you've worked on become a home for someone else.

Like every strategy in real estate investing, flipping isn't for everyone. It requires patience, a knack for spotting potential, and a willingness to get your hands dirty. But for those who relish a challenge and enjoy seeing tangible results, flipping can be a dynamic and lucrative path.

If you choose to walk down this road, remember to arm yourself with knowledge, stay alert to market trends, and always keep your end goal in sight.

Renovating and Renting

Now, let's dive into a strategy that's close to my heart - renovating and renting.

Imagine this: you find a property in a desirable neighborhood that just needs a little TLC. You acquire it, spruce it up, and then rent it out to tenants who are more than willing to pay for the comfort and convenience you've created.

This approach is what we call the "renovate and rent" strategy - a method that can provide consistent cash flow and the potential for property appreciation.

Before we move forward, let me clarify: this strategy is not about buying a property, throwing in a few cosmetic changes and then charging rent. No! It's about finding a property in a great location, breathing new life into it with thoughtful renovations, and turning it into a desirable home for a tenant. It's about creating value.

So why am I a fan of this strategy? Because it's a powerful vehicle for building long-term wealth. You're not just looking for a quick profit here. Instead, you're creating an income stream that keeps flowing, month after month, year after year. That's the beauty of rental income - it doesn't stop!

Now, you're probably wondering what it takes to successfully renovate and rent a property. Well, let me share the three key elements with you:

1. **Good Location:** A desirable neighborhood or location is usually a significant factor for tenants. Proximity to schools, shopping centers, public transportation, and other amenities can add to the property's appeal.

2. **Quality Renovations:** It's not just about renovating; it's about renovating smartly. Focus on improvements that add value, like modern bathrooms, a well-equipped

kitchen, or energy-efficient features. And remember, quality is king!

3. **Effective Property Management:** You're not just a property owner—you're a landlord. Managing a rental property involves finding and retaining good tenants, maintaining the property, and ensuring rent is collected on time.

In my experience, the renovate-and-rent strategy can be an exciting journey. Every property is a new adventure - a chance to breathe life into a home and create something truly valuable.

And the best part? This strategy opens the door to passive income. As the landlord, your role is to maintain the property and ensure your tenants are happy. In return, you enjoy a steady stream of income that can lead to long-term financial freedom.

To sum it up, renovating and renting can be a fantastic path for those looking to invest in single-family properties. It's not just about making a quick buck—it's about building a lasting legacy of wealth. And from where I stand, that's a rewarding journey worth embarking on.

So, among the three paths discussed, which one is right for you? What kind of investor do you want to be? The choice is yours.

Step 5: Marketing to Find Your Property

Finding the perfect property - that's your mission, the star to your wandering ship. It can feel overwhelming at times, like searching for a needle in a haystack. But see, I've been there too. I've felt the thrill, the uncertainty, and ultimately, the satisfaction of finding that perfect single-family property.

I've realized that marketing isn't just about *getting your name out there*. It's more about *making connections* and *building relationships* - it's about creating a network that helps you find those hidden gems. With this in mind, let me share some of my most reliable, time-tested strategies.

Road Signs

When we talk about marketing in real estate, **road signs** often get overlooked. They're old-school, you might say. They're not flashy, they don't have bells and whistles. But don't be fooled by their simplicity - these humble signs are silent yet potent agents in your property hunt.

They've been around us all our lives, guiding us, and leading us to our destinations. In a world drowning in digital noise, they're a breath of fresh air. People notice them, and that's the first step in making a connection.

Now, it's not just about planting these signs anywhere. There's a strategy behind it. *Location* - that's the key. Pinpoint the neighborhoods ripe for real estate opportunities, and let your signs be the beacon for motivated sellers in those areas. Trust me, a well-placed sign can catch the eye of the most elusive sellers.

As important as the location is the message on your sign. Less is more, remember? Keep it crisp and clear, with your contact information being the star of the show. The goal is to make it easy for sellers to reach out to you, to initiate that first, crucial dialogue.

In my years of experience, despite the digital revolution, road signs have remained a tried-and-true method for generating seller leads. They're cost-effective, they're straightforward, and most importantly, they work.

The Direct Mail Method

What makes direct mail stand out is its ability to *target* your desired sellers. You can select specific neighborhoods, property types, or even target owners who might be facing foreclosure. This precision allows you to focus your efforts and resources on the most promising leads - no more shooting in the dark.

Once you've identified your target audience, it's time to create your direct mail. This isn't just a casual note; it's a strategic, thoughtfully composed message designed to catch the attention of potential sellers.

The trick is to keep it simple but compelling. The main message should be about *them,* their needs, and how you can solve their problems. Remember to make your contact information unmistakable and easy to find; after all, you want those sellers to reach out to you.

Online Pay-Per-Click Advertising

In the digital age, we are living in, it's essential to utilize cutting-edge strategies that take advantage of technology's power. One such strategy is **Online Pay-Per-Click Advertising**.

Simply put, pay-per-click (PPC) advertising is an online marketing method where you pay a small fee each time someone clicks on your ad. Think of it as buying visits to your website or landing page, rather than trying to earn those visits organically.

Imagine reaching out to a massive, diverse audience without running up a colossal bill. That's the beauty of PPC advertising. You're only charged when someone clicks your ad, making it an incredibly cost-effective strategy.

Starting a PPC campaign might seem daunting, but trust me, it's worth the initial effort. Begin by identifying your target audience - which neighborhoods, property types, or owner situations are you interested in? Once you've got that figured out, craft a compelling, succinct ad that addresses potential sellers' needs and showcases how you can offer a solution.

Remember, the goal is to pique their interest enough to click on your ad and explore further. Be sure to make your contact information prominent and easy to find - you want those potential sellers to reach out to you!

Print Advertising

Print Advertising - it might seem almost archaic in our digital age, but here's the thing – it's still a potent tool in your real estate investing toolbox. It may not be as flashy as online pay-per-click advertising, but, in my experience, it's had a charm and efficacy of its own.

Let's face it, not everyone is hooked onto their smartphones and computers. Yes, even in this age of digital bombardment, people still look forward to flipping through their local newspapers, penny-savers, and magazines. They enjoy the tactile experience, the smell of the ink, the rustle of the pages - it's a part of their routine, their comfort zone. And that, my friend, is a demographic you don't want to overlook.

When placed thoughtfully, print ads have the power to catch the eye and the mind, leading to that all-important initial conversation. But here's the trick – your ad isn't just an announcement; it's a conversation starter. It's your first connection with a potential seller. It needs to be more than just information – it needs to be an invitation, a call to action.

Your ad should clearly communicate what you're looking for in terms of properties. It should tell a seller that you're there, you're interested, and you're ready to address their needs. Keep it simple, but compelling. Make it easy for them to reach out to you.

Radio Advertising

With radio advertising, you have the potential to tap into a local audience, and that's a big deal. Local means these are people who are invested in their community, who take pride in their neighborhood. They're the ones with a keen eye on the shift in the real estate market. They're your potential leads. A well-crafted radio ad has the power to tap into this local audience, reaching into their homes, their cars, and their lives.

Just like a great pop song, a good radio ad is all about getting the message right. You want to strike the right chords and create a melody that stays with the listener. Your ad should highlight your investment services in a language that's relatable, and accessible. Talk about *why* you're in this business, and why you care about investing in single-family properties. Draw them into your story.

Use your contact information as your catchy chorus. It needs to be simple, memorable, something that sticks with the listener long after your ad has played. A catchy web domain or an easy-to-remember phone number could make all the difference.

Here's the thing: radio advertising isn't about the hard sell; it's about starting a conversation.

Search Engine Optimization (SEO)

Ever wondered how Google decides which results to show you first when you search for something? That's SEO in action. Basically, it's a set of rules and techniques used to optimize your online content so that search engines find it attractive and place it higher in search results.

Let's say you have a website or a blog where you share valuable information about investing in single-family properties. You want potential sellers and leads to find you. But here's the thing: there's a sea of information out there, and your potential leads are likely to get lost in it. SEO is your lighthouse, guiding these folks right to your website.

SEO isn't some mystical, complex beast; it's a tool, and like any tool, it's all about how you use it. Focus on your content. Make it relevant, valuable, and engaging. Use keywords—terms that potential leads are likely to search for. But remember, don't just stuff these words in there. Incorporate them naturally, and make them a part of your narrative.

And, importantly, be patient. SEO isn't a magic wand, and you won't see results overnight. But trust me, when those results start showing, you'll realize it was worth the wait.

Networking with Local Real Estate Professionals

In my years of navigating the fascinating world of real estate investing, I've realized that relationships play a pivotal role. They are the bridges that connect us to opportunities, knowledge, and growth. When you're stepping into the world of real estate investing, especially with single-family properties, one of the smartest moves that I advocate for and you can make is to build relationships with local real estate professionals.

When you're exploring uncharted territories, wouldn't it be helpful to have a local guide, someone who knows the terrain, the ins and outs, and the hidden gems? Local real estate professionals, whether they are realtors, property managers, or wholesalers, have an intimate understanding of the local market. They have their fingers on the pulse of the community. They stay updated on local real estate trends, market dynamics, and potential opportunities. They are your local guides, your allies, in the pursuit of investment opportunities.

When it comes to building these connections, active networking is key. It's not a one-time event, but a journey, a process. It's about showing up, being present, and staying consistent.

Consider attending local real estate events. These are vibrant platforms where you can connect with like-minded individuals, share insights, learn from their experiences, and even find potential collaborations. Join real estate industry organizations that align with your interests. This not only gives you access to a vast network of professionals but also keeps you updated with industry trends, news, and resources.

Remember, networking is not a one-way street. It's not just about what you can gain, but also about what you can contribute. Share your insights, lend a helping hand, be of value to others. This spirit of reciprocity is what nurtures and strengthens these relationships.

Now, I understand that networking can feel daunting, especially if you're just starting out. But trust me, it gets easier, one conversation at a time. Start small, and build gradually. Maybe start by attending a local real estate event or joining online discussion platforms. Remember, every little step counts, and every conversation matters.

Online Listings and Databases

Online real estate listings and databases offer a plethora of options at your fingertips. The beauty of these platforms is their variety. From *Multiple Listing Service* (MLS) to various real estate websites, you're spoilt for choice. The MLS, for instance, is a comprehensive directory that real estate agents use to list properties for sale. A simple search can reveal numerous properties available for sale, complete with photos, descriptions, and price details. Think of it as your online real estate supermarket. For instance, it was the Multiple Listing Service (MLS) that led me to discover my second investment in the form of a single-family home. This investment wasn't just a simple buy, but an exciting opportunity to renovate and resell, adding a splash of creativity and business acumen to the mix.

Here's something to consider: not all properties make it to the limelight of public listings. Some are tucked away in the quieter corners of the internet, away from the public eye. These are known as *off-market properties*. They're typically not publicly advertised (not on the MLS), which makes them a gold mine of untapped opportunities. Access to these properties can give you an edge over other investors who are limited to only publicly listed properties. Take, for instance, my initial venture into the single-family home market. This wasn't just any property; it was an exclusive off-market deal. I seized the opportunity to invest, giving the property a complete renovation facelift and successfully putting it back on the market to resell.

Similarly, foreclosure listings are another resource not to be overlooked. These are properties that have been seized by lenders due to the previous owners' inability to keep up with their mortgage payments. These listings often fly under the radar, yet they can offer some of the best deals. Take for instance the third property I acquired, which was a result of carefully tracking foreclosure listings. This served as a golden opportunity for a 'renovate and rent' investment strategy, transforming the once-distressed property into a lucrative rental.

While these online platforms can be treasure troves, it's important to approach them with a discerning eye. Not all that glitters is gold, and not every listed property is a profitable investment. As a real estate investor, you need to scrutinize each listing, conduct thorough research, and, if possible, I highly recommend visiting the property in person.

In conclusion, I'd like to stress on one of the most important strategies: **consistency and persistence**. Real estate investing is not a one-time deal. It's a continuous process of searching, analyzing, and seizing opportunities as they come. With online listings and databases, the search becomes easier, but it still demands patience and diligence.

In the world of real estate investing, the early bird does catch the worm. So, keep an eye on these platforms. Check for updates regularly. Remember, a good investment opportunity doesn't wait for anyone.

Step 6: What is Your Budget?

Your budget isn't just a number on a spreadsheet or an approximate amount you're willing to spend—it's the backbone of your investment strategy. It's the line in the sand that dictates how far we can go with our real estate investments and can make or break your foray into the world of real estate investing.

Let's reframe our perspective before we move on: envision your budget not as a limitation, but rather as a passport to freedom. This freedom empowers you to make strategic, well-informed decisions, using comparable properties as benchmarks, propelling you towards your objectives with confidence and clarity.

Understanding Your Financial Resources

In the realm of real estate investing, money matters. It's like the fuel that keeps your investment journey going. But don't be disheartened. Remember, it's not about having a fat bank account—it's about managing the resources effectively. Think of it like a health check for your finances.

Let's start with the basics. The first thing to consider is your available cash. This is your immediate weapon in the market. It's the capital that you can use to kickstart your investments, without having to worry about repayments or interest rates. The more you have, the more you can invest. But don't be disheartened if your savings account isn't overflowing right now. Like every seed that grows into a towering tree, every investor begins their journey from modest beginnings. When I embarked on my investment adventure, I was far from financially robust. My savings account was non-existent, and a humble sum of $1,000 was all that I could claim in my checking account. Yet, these humble beginnings did not deter my ambitions, instead they nurtured my first acquisition - a single-family property.

Next up is credit. This is your secret partner—one that will silently back you up when you need it. A good credit score can be a game-changer in your real estate investment journey. It can provide you access to loans, mortgages, and other financing options. But also, managing your credit effectively is key. It's like a trust score, telling lenders that you're a reliable person to loan money to. My credit was good enough to finance my first investment property.

Lastly, let's dive into investment financing. Think of it as your very own booster rocket, launching you deep into the cosmos of real estate investing. The secret ingredient here is OPM - leveraging Other People's Money to supercharge your investments. Instead of solely relying on my personal funds, I champion the use of OPM whenever feasible. This could materialize in the form of loans, mortgages, or even synergistic partnerships with fellow investors. The wider your access to financing, the broader your investment horizon. However, a word of caution: this is a powerful tool and must be handled with care. It's crucial to oversee this judiciously to ensure its waves lift you, not drown you. Recalling Step 2 of this book, my initial foray into single-family property investing was made possible by financing 80% of the deal through a local bank and sourcing the remaining 20% via a Home Equity Line of Credit (HELOC) from my personal residence.

Every individual's financial resources are unique, just like fingerprints. So, it's important to understand them well. Knowing your financial resources will help you envision your investment path. It will dictate the kind of properties you can afford, the risks you can take, and the goals you can achieve. Seeing the bigger picture and understanding your financial resources can make the difference between success and failure in real estate investing.

Budgeting for Renovation Projects

Picture this: a house, sitting humble and worn out, yearning for a touch of grace and a dash of charm. It's not just a house—it's a blank canvas, a field of possibility, and it's waiting for an artist's hand to transform it into a masterpiece.

But before you don your tool belt and swap your pen for a paintbrush, let's get one thing straight: a successful makeover isn't just about creativity—it's about careful budgeting and meticulous planning.

Material Costs

The first stop on this journey is material costs. Just like the chef needs the finest ingredients to whip up a culinary delight, you need quality materials to build a dream home. Lumber, fixtures, appliances, finishing materials—they're not just inanimate objects, but the very bones and veins of your real estate investment. Remember, *quality matters more than quantity*. I've seen far too many investors opt for cheap, subpar materials to cut corners, only to have it backfire down the line.

Labor Costs

Next, we have the labor costs. You're the general here, but you'll need an army of professionals to execute your vision. Contractors, electricians, plumbers—you name it. They're your silent partners, the backstage crew who help bring the magic to life. It might be tempting to skimp on labor costs, but let me tell you from experience, *you get what you pay for*. My experience with the garage renovation I mentioned in Step 3 is an apt example. Initially, I opted for an affordable contractor to save some bucks. However, this decision backfired so badly that I had to let the contractor go, which, ironically, proved costlier in the end. Such was the magnitude of this disaster that the contractor earned the nickname *"cobbler"*, a tag I now use to describe sub-par work. Therefore, it's wise to invest in high-quality, dependable labor. *Quality*, reliable labor might cost a tad more, but the assurance and peace of mind it brings is priceless.

Permit Costs

Third on the list, the permit costs. You'll need to do your homework here, research local permitting requirements, and budget for any associated fees. It might seem like a tedious task, but trust me, it's better to first have all your ducks in a row than face costly violations later on.

Contingency Funds

Now, let's talk about contingency funds—a topic close to my heart. You can prepare for the known, but the unknown lurks in the shadows. *Unexpected expenses are not a question of 'if', but 'when'.* That's where contingency funds come in. They're your safety net, your buffer against the unexpected. Always, always include them in your budget.

Overhead Expenses

Overhead expenses, insurance, utilities, property taxes, loan interest during the renovation period—I've seen many an investor overlook these, only to get a rude shock later. Remember, *it's the little things that add up*.

Financing Costs

And finally, we come to financing costs. If you're using financing, be sure to account for interest payments and fees associated with your loans. This will help you determine whether the return on your investment makes it worthwhile, or if you should look for other options.

Every single-family property investor's journey has a unique story, and every renovation project is a world of its own. As the author of your own investing journey, it's essential to balance your budget and your vision. Remember: *ambition is admirable, but without a sensible budget, it's like a ship without a lighthouse—bound to crash on the rocky shores.*

Analyzing ROI in Real Estate Investment

As a seasoned real estate investor, I've seen the highs and lows that come with the territory. I've watched the market fluctuate, felt the adrenaline of closing a deal, and experienced the gratification of transforming a worn-out property into a family's dream home. But let's be honest, at the end of the day, investing in real estate is about making a profit. And this brings us to the crucial concept of **Return on Investment or ROI**.

In simple terms, ROI indicates how much money you stand to make on your investment. Now, the question is: How do we calculate ROI? What factors should we consider? Is the process the same for every investment? As your guide and fellow investor, let me take you through the different scenarios and how ROI plays a pivotal role in each.

The Wholesaling Strategy

Picture yourself as a wholesaler, the middleman who discovers undervalued properties and contracts them to other investors or buyers, making a profit in the process. The formula for ROI in this strategy is straightforward—the difference between the contract price and the contract assignment fee.

But remember, as a wholesaler, you're also a marketer trying to create a win-win situation for both the seller and the buyer. Therefore, marketing costs are a vital part of your expenses, impacting your ROI.

The "Fix and Flip" Strategy

Here's where things get interesting. As an investor, you have the power to transform a house—infuse life into its worn-out walls, fix its creaking doors, and polish its aged floors. But all of this comes with a cost. In fact, the "Fix and Flip" strategy involves several costs—purchase price, renovation costs, holding costs, and eventually, the selling price.

Your ROI is derived from the formula [(Net Profit / Total Investment) x 100]. So, invest your time in determining whether this strategy would be profitable for your chosen property. Remember, every house has a story, and it's your job to unravel its potential.

The "Renovate and Rent" Strategy

Imagine becoming the owner of a property, renovating it, and then renting it out. Not only does it sound exciting, but it also offers the potential for long-term passive income. The ROI in this case is calculated based on the rental income and the property's appreciation potential.

Don't forget about property management, maintenance, and property taxes. The key lies in balancing these expenses with your rental income and property appreciation.

Understanding ROI isn't rocket science, but it requires a fair amount of knowledge and an analytical mind. In my experience, the investors who truly succeed are those who diligently calculate and analyze ROI before diving into any single-family investment property.

Step 7: Property Valuation and Deal Analysis

This step is the proverbial fork in the road. It's where you either make a smart, well-informed investment or end up with a money pit that drains your resources.

Contrary to popular belief, real estate is not always about location, location, location. No, it's also about understanding the potential value of a property and the cost of bringing that value to fruition. Think of it like a rough diamond. The value is there, hidden in the stone. It's your job to polish it, to bring out its brilliance.

Determining Property Value

Valuing a property is more of an art than a science. It's a process that can sometimes feel nebulous, uncertain. However, it's not as daunting as it seems if you understand the basics and have the right tools at your disposal.

So, how do we determine the value of a property? Well, there are several methods that we can use. The first of these is called **Comparative Market Analysis (CMA).** This involves comparing the property you're interested in to similar properties that have recently sold in the area. It's like comparing apples to apples to figure out if you're getting a good deal.

CMA is mostly done by **professional appraisals.** These are conducted by licensed appraisers who are well-versed in evaluating properties. They examine a number of factors including the condition of the house, the neighborhood, and recent sales of comparable properties.

Lastly, CMA can also be done by yourself. It's also a method of **researching recent comparable sales** in the area. This is a more hands-on approach where you dig into property records and sales data yourself. This can be time-consuming, but it's also a great way to get a comprehensive understanding of the local market.

Creating Value through Renovation

Think about the last time you walked into a beautifully renovated home. The gleaming hardwood floors, the freshly painted walls, the modern kitchen, all working together to create an ambiance of comfort and luxury. It's this kind of transformation that can significantly boost the value of a property and make it a magnet for interested buyers or tenants.

Remember, perception is the key. You're not just renovating a house—you're building a home. A place that tells a story, that resonates with people's aspirations.

However, while making renovations is exciting, it's crucial to approach them strategically. Throwing money at a property and hoping its value increases is not a guaranteed strategy. Not all upgrades are created equal, and not all of them will yield a satisfactory return on investment.

The right kind of renovation is one that brings you closer to your property's potential value, not further away. For instance, cosmetic improvements can be a game-changer—they're generally affordable, quick to implement, and can significantly enhance the property's appeal.

In today's eco-conscious world, energy-efficient upgrades are more than just a trendy buzzword—they're a tangible selling point. Installing solar panels or upgrading to energy-efficient appliances can attract buyers or tenants who value sustainability and are willing to pay a premium for it.

Consider this: energy efficiency is not just about saving money on utilities—it's about creating a sustainable living environment. It speaks volumes about the kind of landlord or seller you are, and the quality of life you're offering.

Sometimes, value creation goes beyond aesthetics and energy efficiency—it requires digging deeper. This could mean enhancing the structure of the property, such as adding an extra bathroom or expanding the living space. Yes, these upgrades may be a bit more costlier. Still, they can significantly increase the property's worth and make it more attractive to families looking for additional space.

Renovation is an opportunity to breathe life into a single-family property. It's your chance to shape its story, enhance its appeal, and unlock its potential value. It's not just about slapping on a fresh coat of paint—it's about crafting a home that people aspire to live in.

Understanding After Repair Value (ARV)

Every real estate investor needs to understand the concept of After Repair Value (ARV).

ARV, or After Repair Value, represents a property's estimated value after all the necessary repairs and renovations are done. It's like a glimpse into your property's future; a future where that fixer-upper you're eyeing transforms into a charming, modern home.

But why is ARV so critical? Well, the answer lies in its direct connection to your potential profits. See, the ARV helps you determine if a particular property is worth investing in. It's the keystone in the arch of your investment strategy.

Imagine walking into a single-family property that needs extensive work. You know there'll be costs – the renovation, the carrying cost during the renovation period, and the cost of the initial purchase. But, here's the million-dollar question: *Will the final value of the property, the ARV, justify these costs?*

Suppose the ARV is significantly higher than your total costs. In that case, you're looking at a good investment opportunity. However, if the ARV is lower, the property might be a money pit that could suck your resources dry.

Now that you understand the importance of ARV, it's critical to also grasp that your profits are as accurate as your ARV calculation. Calculating ARV can be a bit tricky, but it's a skill that gets better with practice and experience.

Maximum Allowable Offer (MAO) Formula

How much should you offer for ta property? And that's where the Maximum Allowable Offer (MAO) formula comes into play.

When it comes to real estate investing, the MAO formula can be your guiding compass. The formula takes into account your desired profit margin and estimated renovation costs. The MAO formula reads like this:

[(ARV X 0.70) - (Cost Estimate of Repairs + Closing Costs + Holding Costs)]

At first glance, it may seem a little complicated, but once you delve deep and understand each component, it's as easy as pie.

Let's break it down, shall we?

The first part of the formula, **ARV X 0.70,** represents the After Repair Value (ARV) of the property, multiplied by 0.70. Why multiply by 0.70, you ask? Well, that's to account for your profit and all the costs associated with buying, holding, and selling the property. It's a slice of the real estate pie that ensures you remain profitable.

The second part of the formula, **Cost Estimate of Repairs + Closing Costs + Holding Costs,** is all about the expenses associated with the property. It includes the cost of necessary repairs, the closing costs of the purchase transaction, and the holding costs (like insurance, property taxes, and interest) you'll incur while owning the property.

Summing up these costs and subtracting them from the first part gives you the MAO, the maximum amount you should consider offering for the property.

Let's take an example. Suppose you come across a single-family investment property with an estimated ARV of $400,000. You've determined that you'll need to spend around $60,000 on repairs. The closing costs are $4,200, and you estimate six months of holding costs to be around $6,000.

Using the MAO formula, the maximum offer would be:

$$[(400,000 \times 0.70) - (60,000 + 4,200 + 6,000)] = \$209,800.$$

Therefore, according to the MAO formula, your maximum offer for this property should be roughly $210,000.

Understanding and correctly using the MAO formula is the secret to success in real estate investing. But remember, it's just a tool to guide you. In the end, the decision lies in your hands. As with any investment, due diligence is crucial—you need to inspect the property thoroughly, understand the local market, and consult with industry experts.

Estimating Repair Costs

"The devil is in the details" – this couldn't be truer for renovation costs. Without a thorough and accurate estimate of repairs, your budget can spiral out of control before you know it. You don't want to end up in a situation where the costs outweigh

the potential returns, turning your promising investment into a money pit. Remember, **your profitability hinges on your ability to keep the repair costs under control.**

Breaking Down the Key Areas

Now, let's roll up our sleeves and consider the key areas that typically need attention during a repair or renovation project.

Plumbing, Electrical, HVAC are the heart and lungs of your property. If they don't function properly, the most stunning aesthetics won't save it. Therefore, ensure the plumbing is leak-free, the electrical system is safe, and the Heating, Ventilation, and Air Conditioning (HVAC) system is working efficiently. Repairs or replacements could be needed, and these costs can be significant, so plan accordingly.

The structural integrity of a property is paramount. Neglecting this aspect could lead to serious issues down the line. Check the roof for leaks or signs of wear, examine the siding for any damage, and ensure the foundation is strong and stable. Remember, these aren't just cosmetic fixes. They're about ensuring the property is safe and secure for its future inhabitants. In my experience I've found that inspecting a property on a rainy day is a great way to see if there is any potential damage from leaks in the roof, siding or foundation.

Windows and doors are not just about keeping the weather out and providing security; they're one of the first things that potential buyers or tenants notice. A well-maintained garage can be a significant selling point for those who value storage or have vehicles. Consider the cost of updating or repairing these elements to enhance the property's curb appeal and functionality.

Never underestimate the power of first impressions. A fresh coat of paint, well-kept landscaping, and clean surroundings can work wonders in enhancing the property's overall appeal. These are relatively inexpensive improvements but can significantly impact how quickly your property attracts buyers or renters.

The interior of a property tells a story to those stepping inside. Old appliances, damaged drywall, worn-out flooring, or outdated tiles can make a disappointing chapter in that story. Upgrades or replacements in these areas can elevate the aesthetic appeal and functionality of the property.

In the end, the art of real estate investment is all about balance – balancing costs with expectations, balancing the current property state with its future potential, and most importantly, balancing your investor instincts with judicious decision-making.

As you gain experience, you'll become more adept at making these cost estimations.

Calculating Potential Profit

This probably goes without saying, but I'll say it anyway - *profit is the lifeblood of investing*. It's the reward you get for the time, effort, and money you put into your single-family property. But here's the thing - the path to profit isn't always clear. I've seen many enthusiastic investors, driven by the lure of quick returns, dive headfirst into a deal without figuring out their potential profits. And you know where that leads them? Down a rabbit hole of unexpected costs, overruns, and at times, substantial financial loss.

Trust me, you don't want to be that investor. You want to be the one who knows his way, who can navigate the twists and turns of real estate investing with confidence. And that, my friend, comes from the power of knowledge – knowledge of your potential profit!

So how do we go about calculating potential profit? It's actually simpler than you might think.

First, you need to figure out the **purchase price** - the initial investment you'll be making to acquire the property. Next, there's the **renovation costs**. When you buy a single-family property with the intention of investing, you'll likely need to make some renovations. Don't forget the **holding costs,** which include things like property taxes and insurance.

Then, there are the **selling costs**. When you're ready to sell the house, you'll likely need to pay a realtor's commission. Finally, your desired **profit margin** is the cushion you build in to ensure you get a return on your investment.

The goal here is to maximize the joy and minimize the regret. And that's exactly what effective profit calculation does. It gives you a reality check, a clear picture of your journey's end before you even begin. If the numbers look promising, you're on to a potential winner. But if they don't, you have the chance to reconsider, to reevaluate your options before it's too late.

Whether it's understanding the importance of ARV, calculating your MAO, accurately estimating repair costs, or calculating potential profits, each component plays a vital role in shaping your investment strategy and trajectory. Remember, real estate isn't just about buying and selling properties—it's about recognizing the potential in a structure, breathing new life into it, and crafting a space that people aspire to call home.

Step 8: Manage Your Team, Budget, and Timeline

Real estate investing *isn't just about properties and profits.* It's about *people, processes,* and *persistence.* It's a world where organizational skills are as valuable as financial acumen. You don't just invest in a property. You invest in your team, you invest your time, and you learn to manage your budget like a seasoned pro. Let's take a walk along the path of **effective management** in real estate investing, a path that will lead you to your destination - success.

The Art of Coordination and Communication

Let's take a journey down the path that's less talked about, but perhaps one of the most crucial aspects of real estate investing: **Coordination and Communication.**

Regular team meetings are a non-negotiable component of successful real estate investing.

Why? Because it's during these meetings that the magic happens. We discuss the journey so far, trace the path ahead, brainstorm on the obstacles, and celebrate the milestones. Every team member gets to share their individual progress, the challenges they faced, and the goals they're aiming for. It's these discussions that ensure we're not just a team, but a team that's all sailing in the same direction.

Now, onto the next piece of our puzzle: **clear expectations**. It's like knowing your part in a play. If the actors aren't clear on their roles, the performance is bound to be in chaos, isn't it? Similarly, in a team, every member needs to know what they're accountable for.

From the onset, clearly communicate your expectations, delineate roles, and define responsibilities for each member. Make it as crystal clear as the water in a pristine lake. Doing this doesn't just establish an environment of accountability, but it also fosters transparency and collaboration. It's like giving each team member their own script in the play of success.

Next up, let's talk about something as simple as **timely updates**. I can't emphasize enough how pivotal they are. It's like the regular health checkups that ensure our bodies are functioning correctly. Timely updates ensure your investment venture is healthy.

Encourage each team member to regularly update you on their tasks, progress, and even the tiniest roadblocks they encounter. This not only helps in early identification and quick resolution of issues but also aids in making timely course corrections. Because remember, in the journey of real estate investing, prevention is always better than cure!

Practicing these principles is like laying a solid foundation for your property - a foundation that will stand the test of time and lead your project to success.

Effective Project Management

I understand that you might find project management to be a daunting task. But trust me, once you get the hang of it, you'll see it's just about staying organized and keeping a keen eye on the details. Let's break it down into manageable chunks.

The Importance of Timelines in Project Management

Creating a solid timeline is the first step towards success in your real estate investing journey. Imagine your project as a journey by train - your timeline is the railway track guiding you towards your destination. A well-structured timeline not only keeps you on track but also helps prevent derailment!

Let's say, you've just bought a single-family property that needs renovation before it hits the market. List down all tasks, no matter how small, and assign a deadline for each. This could include tasks like obtaining renovation permits, hiring a contractor, completing the renovation, staging the house, and so on.

Remember, your timeline is your roadmap. It's dynamic and flexible. If a task gets delayed, adjust your timeline accordingly. The key is to keep moving forward, no matter the pace.

Keeping Your Finances in Check

Next up: **Budget management**. Would you go grocery shopping without checking your wallet? I guess not! And that's the principle you should apply to your real estate investing project as well. Keeping a close eye on your budget ensures you don't overspend and stay within your financial limits.

Make it a habit to regularly track your expenses. Did the renovation cost more than you anticipated? Adjust your budget or find other areas where you can cut back. It's all about balance. Budget management is not about depriving; it's about making informed decisions.

Navigating through Issues

In your real estate investment journey, you'll undoubtedly encounter obstacles. But don't fret - **tackling issues head-on** is the secret to smooth sailing. Whether it's a sudden hike in material costs, delays in renovation, or changes in market dynamics, a swift response minimizes disruptions and keeps your project on track.

Every issue you resolve is a stepping stone towards your project's success. Think of it this way - each problem solved is one less roadblock in your path.

Procurement

Lastly, let's talk about **procurement**. Efficient procurement of necessary supplies is often overlooked but is essential to keep your project on track and within budget.

Start by building relationships with reliable suppliers. Just like you'd prefer buying from a grocer you trust, it's essential to have suppliers who you know will deliver quality materials on time and at competitive prices.

Keep track of your inventory. Running out of materials in the middle of a renovation is a nightmare you want to avoid. Lastly, don't shy away from exploring different sourcing options. There's always a deal waiting for you, be it bulk purchases, discounts, or online marketplaces.

Navigating Permits and Regulations

I've seen many bright-eyed investors dive headfirst into the renovation process, only to be brought to a screeching halt by the heavy hand of the law. You'd be surprised how often people overlook the importance of permits and regulations.

Digging into the Research

Research. It's not the most exciting part of the process, but it's critical. Similarly you should never start a renovation project without understanding your local building codes, zoning regulations, and permit requirements.

Your local city or county website would be a good starting point. If it seems overwhelming, consider reaching out to a local contractor or real estate attorney. Their expertise can save you time and help avoid costly mistakes.

Permit Applications

Once you've got a grip on the requirements, it's time to apply for the necessary permits. It's a step you absolutely **cannot skip.** Sure, it can be tedious and time-consuming. But remember, rushing through this stage could lead to fines, legal issues, and even demolition orders. It's far better to invest your time now than to pay the price later—literally.

The Inspections

Now, with permits in hand, you're almost ready to get started on your project. But there's one more checkpoint to cross: inspections.

Inspections are mandatory and are conducted at various stages of your project to ensure compliance with safety and building standards. It's like your car's occasional check-ups to ensure everything's running smoothly. Annoying? Maybe. Necessary? Absolutely.

Consider scheduling your inspections well in advance to avoid delays. And remember, passing these inspections is a testament to the quality of your work.

Embracing the Challenge

I won't sugarcoat it—navigating permits and regulations can be challenging. But remember, every challenge is an opportunity in disguise. By diligently following these steps, you're not just adhering to the law; you're also ensuring the safety and longevity of your investment.

Real estate investing is a multifaceted journey that requires more than just financial prowess. It's about managing your team effectively, which involves clear communication, certain expectations, and timely updates. Project management forms the backbone, where a well-thought-out timeline and strict budget management can make all the difference. Navigating through issues with a calm and rational approach, efficient procurement, and a thorough understanding of permits and regulations are all vital aspects. This journey, while challenging, is a pathway to success, and by implementing these key strategies, you're renovating not only properties but a robust and resilient investment business.

Step 9: Time for Your Exit

The moment you've been working towards, the final stretch, is just as important as the initial steps you took when you plunged into this venture. So, let's discuss "Your Exit" – that crucial juncture when your project approaches conclusion and you begin to contemplate the best ways to realize the fruits of your labor.

Indeed, the finish line might be in sight, but the journey is far from over. This is the stage where you need to focus on your exit strategy. There are a few paths you can take. For instance, you might opt to 'wholesale' the property – selling it to another investor. Alternatively, you might decide to resell the property yourself, perhaps to a homeowner. Or, you may choose to rent out the property and enjoy a steady stream of income.

In my years of experience, I've found that an effective combination of marketing and negotiation skills can command profitable deals, no matter the path you choose. Yet, it's important not to rush this decision. Instead, weigh your options and consider how each aligns with the objectives you set at the beginning of this journey.

Wholesaling Strategies

As we have already discussed, wholesaling means taking on a middleman role where you enter into a contract to buy a single-family property and then assign that contract to another investor or buyer, for a fee.

The success of your wholesaling endeavor largely depends on the strength of your network. This network should ideally consist of investors, buyers, and even real estate investment groups who are actively in the market for single-family properties. Online platforms could also prove to be a goldmine for potential buyers.

Remember, a wider network increases the likelihood of you finding the perfect match for your property. It's like casting a wider net into the sea, you're bound to catch more fish.

Analyzing the Property: A Crucial Step

Every single-family property you come across is like a story waiting to be discovered. Some might be in distress, others might have immense potential hidden underneath, waiting to be uncovered. Your job is to find these properties and assess their potential for wholesaling based on the market demand and your network's preferences.

Negotiation is the key to unlock the best possible deals in wholesaling. It's the music that sets the tone for the dance of real estate dealing. Mastering the art of negotiation is like learning to play a musical instrument - you start with the basics, practice relentlessly and gradually you compose your own symphony. In the world of wholesaling, you'll be negotiating with both, the seller to secure the contract, and the buyer to agree on the assignment fee.

Wholesaling, like any other investment strategy, comes with its own set of risks and rewards. It's like surfing, you need to ride the wave just right. A misjudgment could lead to a wipeout, but if done right, it can be an exhilarating experience. Therefore, tread carefully, make informed decisions, and always keep your eyes on the prize.

In the end, whether wholesaling is the right path for you or not, depends entirely on your personal circumstances and preferences. But remember, real estate is more than just a game of numbers; it's a journey filled with opportunities, learnings, and growth.

Reselling Strategies

Reselling is not just about buying a property and selling it for a profit. Instead, I like to think of it as an opportunity to breathe new life into a space that might have been neglected or overlooked. We've already discussed this as a 'fix-and-flip'. Let's dive deeper into it.

Strategy is key. You can't just dive in, hammer in hand, hoping for the best. An efficient and cost-effective renovation requires a well-thought-out plan, with each step meticulously mapped out. Ask yourself, what changes will make the most significant impact? What upgrades will be most attractive to potential buyers?

I like to focus on the heart of the home - the kitchen and bathrooms. A modern, stylish kitchen can do wonders for the overall appeal of the house. Similarly, updated bathrooms speak volumes about the care and attention you've put into the property. Always remember, however, to keep things within budget. *Extravagance shouldn't come at the expense of profitability.*

My years in real estate have taught me one crucial lesson: timing is everything. Keep tabs on the market, and know when it's in your favor. Is it a buyer's market or a seller's market? Depending on your area, seasonality could also play a role.

For instance, families usually prefer to move during the summer, between school years. Keep these factors in mind when you plan your exit strategy. Remember, *the perfect time to sell can significantly boost your profit margin.*

Once your property is ready to shine, it's time to show it to the world. Your marketing strategy should be as carefully crafted as your renovation plan. Leverage online platforms, and don't underestimate the power of compelling visuals. Professional photographs that highlight the property's features are a must.

Consider also hosting virtual tours. In today's tech-savvy world, they're an excellent way to engage potential buyers. Remember, every detail counts. From the wording of your listing to the quality of your photographs, every element contributes to the narrative you are creating for your property. *A well-marketed home can capture the hearts and minds of potential buyers and command a higher selling price.*

Reselling can be a profitable adventure, but it's not without its risks. The capital investment is significantly higher than wholesaling, and the process can be lengthier and more complex. However, with careful planning, a keen eye for detail, and the right strategies, you can maximize your profits while creating a dream home for someone else.

Renting Strategies

Let's shift our focus now to a different approach, one that may resonate with your inner long-term planner. Allow me to introduce you to the concept of *renting strategies*. Renting, as an exit strategy, can provide a steady stream of income and turn your single-family home into a veritable cash cow.

Conjure this image in your mind: a tenant who pays rent on time, maintains the property with care, and coexists peacefully with the neighborhood. This ideal tenant isn't a myth, but they're not always easy to find. The secret lies in *rigorous tenant screening*. Always remember to conduct thorough background checks, credit checks, and employment verification. I once had a tenant who looked great on paper, but I got a hunch and decided to call his previous landlord. As it turned out, he had a history of late payments and I saved myself a potential headache.

Now, let's talk about *property management*. Do you roll up your sleeves and get to work, or do you hire a professional? If you love the thrill of hands-on work, you're welcome to manage the property yourself. But, if the thought of addressing plumbing issues at midnight sends shivers down your spine, it may be worth considering a property management company.

Imagine this, your property is ready, your ideal tenant is interested, and then they ask about the rent. You need to have this answer ready, and it should be a number that compensifies your efforts and aligns with the current market. In my early days, I made the mistake of pricing my property too high, which led to vacancies, and too low, which cut into my profits. After a few trials and errors, I realized the importance of a thorough *market analysis* to determine the most competitive rental rates.

Renting, as you can see, is an art and a science. It requires careful consideration, meticulous planning, and a fair bit of gut instinct. It's not a strategy to be chosen lightly, but it can be hugely rewarding if done right. Remember, *knowledge is power,* and the more you understand about these strategies, the more likely you are to make an informed decision that aligns with your investment goals. Whether it's wholesaling, reselling, or renting, the path you choose is a reflection of your investment style and personal goals. I'm here to guide you, but ultimately, the choice is yours. *Your real estate journey is waiting for you!*

Marketing Your Single-Family Property

Selling is storytelling.

No matter what exit strategy you take, marketing is going to be the key to success. And with that, let's dive into the mesmerizing world of marketing.

Part 1: The Power of Online Listings

Remember when we used to flip through the Yellow Pages to find a service or product? Well, times have certainly changed.

Today, the world is at our fingertips, and the internet is our new Yellow Pages.

In my years of experience, I've found that websites like *MLS, Zillow, and Realtor.com* are magnificent platforms for property listings. But simply uploading your property's information and hitting 'post' won't cut it. I want you to envision your listing as the first chapter of your property's story.

Here's a trick I often use - I imagine myself as a potential buyer and think about what I'd like to see in a listing. High-quality photographs are a must, showcasing every room, the exterior, and unique features. A picture, after all, is worth a thousand words. But, don't let the images do all the talking. Pen down a detailed, vibrant description. Highlight the home's best features, but also paint a picture of what life could be like in the property. Remember, you're not just selling bricks and mortar; you're selling a lifestyle.

Part 2: The Art of Staging

Let's move on to a concept that's often overlooked but can make a world of difference in how your property is perceived - *staging*. Picture this: you walk into an empty house with bare walls, cold, dark corners, and a vacant echo. Now imagine the same space, but with cozy furniture, warm lighting, and a welcoming atmosphere. Which would you prefer?

Staging a home is like preparing the stage for a play. It provides context and helps potential buyers envision the property as their future home. A well-staged home often commands higher prices, and I've seen properties sell faster when they're staged right. You don't necessarily need to splurge on this; sometimes, a little decluttering, good lighting, and strategic furniture placement can go a long way.

Part 3: The Charm of Open Houses

Finally, let's discuss a time-tested, classic marketing strategy: the *open house*. There's something beautifully tangible about an open house. It's an opportunity for interested parties to physically explore the property, feel its energy, and envision themselves living in the space.

Hosting an open house requires planning and attention to detail. Make sure the property is clean, well-lit, and inviting. Be present to answer questions and highlight the key features of the property. Greet every visitor with a smile; your warmth and enthusiasm can be infectious.

Remember, an open house is more than just a tour; it's a conversation between you, the potential buyer, and the property. Listen to the visitors' feedback; it can provide valuable insights into what they're looking for and how your property meets (or can be tweaked to meet) their needs.

To sum it up, marketing a single-family property isn't just about putting it up for sale; it's about weaving a compelling narrative and creating an irresistible proposition for potential buyers or tenants. It's about telling your property's story in a way that resonates with people and makes them want to be a part of it.

The key to successful marketing lies in understanding your audience and crafting a strategy that speaks to them. So, roll up your sleeves, put on your creative hat, and let your property shine!

Negotiating and Closing Deals: The Art of Real Estate

The Power of Negotiation

Imagine this: It's a sunny day, and you're standing across the table from a seller, discussing a charming single-family property you've had your eyes on. The conversation is cordial, but you're aware of the underlying dance taking place - the dance of negotiation.

Negotiation isn't about 'winning' or 'losing'; it's about arriving at a win-win situation that aligns with both parties' interests. As a real estate investor, you're not just buying a property;

you're creating relationships, connecting with people, and making decisions that will impact your financial future. *Hone your negotiation skills.* Listen more than you talk, understand the other person's perspective, and don't forget to always, always, maintain your integrity.

Due Diligence: Your Safety Net

Now, let's talk about due diligence. I like to think of due diligence as the 'safety net' in a real estate deal. It's what keeps you grounded when the excitement of a new investment opportunity takes flight.

Thinking back to my early days in real estate, I remember the eagerness to close a deal, often overlooking crucial details. One such instance was overlooking an important title search, which later led to complications. It was a valuable lesson: *Always conduct thorough due diligence.*

In the world of real estate, due diligence encompasses everything from title searches and inspections to financing and legalities. It's about delving deeper, peering beneath the surface, and understanding what you're truly getting into.

Closing Coordination: The Grand Finale

And finally, we have the grand finale - closing the deal. If negotiation is the dance and due diligence is the safety net, then closing is the final bow that concludes the performance. Closing a deal requires coordination. It entails working closely with your real estate agent, attorney, or title company to ensure everything aligns perfectly.

The documents need to be in order, the money needs to transfer smoothly, and all parties have to be on board. Closing a deal is an exciting moment, but it also requires attention and care. *Make sure you triple-check everything before signing on the dotted line.*

I recall one of my first closing experiences; feeling a mix of excitement and apprehension. It was a complex process, but seeing it come to fruition was immensely satisfying. From then on, I knew that *successful coordination could make or break a deal.*

Remember, flexibility and adaptability are key to successful real estate investing. What worked for one property might not work for another. Stay open to possibilities, learn from your experiences, and above all, enjoy the journey.

As you embark on your real estate adventure, remember that every deal, every negotiation, and every closing is a stepping stone towards your investing goals. And remember, I'm here, sharing my insights and experiences, to help guide you along the way.

By embracing negotiation, due diligence, and closing coordination, you're not just investing in properties; you're investing in your future. Here's to successful deals and prosperous investments!

Step 10: Celebrate, Learn, Move Forward, and Repeat the Process

As you round up one project and prepare to step into the next, it's time to pause, rejoice, and revel in your accomplishments, regardless of their magnitude. This is the moment to reflect, learn from the journey, and then carry those lessons into your next venture.

After all, real estate investing is a vibrant, dynamic landscape where learning and growth are ongoing processes. Success isn't a destination in this realm - it's an exhilarating journey you embark upon, time and again. Let's dive deeper into this!

Isn't it fascinating to look back at your journey, to marvel at how far you've come from where you started? It's these moments of introspection that are integral to your growth and improvement as a real estate investor.

Set aside some time to reflect on your journey - the humble beginnings, the milestones achieved, and the hurdles you've leaped over. This introspection won't just help keep a spring in your step - it'll also serve as a light for your path ahead. By maintaining a positive outlook and staying motivated, you'll find yourself savoring the fruits of your hard-earned success.

In the world of real estate investing, every achievement - big or small - is cause for a grand celebration. It could be closing a deal successfully, reaching a particular financial milestone, or wrapping up a renovation project within the stipulated time and budget.

Giving yourself a well-deserved pat on the back for these victories imparts a lasting motivation - one that'll keep you committed to this exciting process. Let's face it - who doesn't love a good celebration?

Of course, not every venture in real estate investing goes according to plan. But that's okay - because every stumble, every setback, and every mistake comes with its own silver lining - a lesson to be learned.

When setbacks occur, instead of dwelling on the negative, take a moment to analyze what went wrong and why. It's these very experiences that can serve as your best teachers, helping you avoid similar obstacles down the line. After all, in the world of real estate investing, every mistake is a stepping stone to greater success.

The journey does not end with one successful deal or even a string of them. The real adventure lies in the endless opportunities ahead, in the forests of future investments that await your exploration.

Goal setting is the compass that guides this expedition. Establishing new investment objectives, the stars you wish to reach, is a ritual I've learned to embrace consistently. You may find yourself longing for a portfolio of single-family properties, or yearning to generate a certain level of rental income.

Perhaps you're drawn to the thrill of venturing into newer domains and exploring new markets. Take a moment to think about those stars you're reaching toward, and then set your course accordingly.

Once you've set your sails, it's imperative to constantly survey the landscape - the shifting **market trends** - to stay ahead.

Understanding the undercurrents of the market, recognizing emerging opportunities, and identifying potential hotspots are fundamental to your journey.

Let me share a snippet from my own quest: I once encountered a promising property in an area touted to be 'the next big thing.' My research, however, revealed a lack of essential amenities and poor public transportation. I decided against investing, and a year later, the area's growth turned out to be a bubble that swiftly burst. The lesson here? Never underestimate the importance of comprehensive market research.

The ocean of real estate investing can be unpredictable. I've seen tranquil waters turn stormy in a flash. Thus, having a sturdy lifeboat - a solid **financial plan** - is crucial to navigate these volatile seas.

Your journey might lead you towards the allure of a mansion, while your lifeboat can only manage a small cottage. That's when you revisit your financial plan. Regularly evaluating your financial situation, checking the strength of your lifeboat, ensures you're equipped to ride the waves of any storm.

In the end, it isn't about making grand gestures but calculated moves. Adjustments to your financial plan, aligned with your investment goals, ensure you have not just the vision but also the means to seize new opportunities that come your way.

Let me tell you a little secret: the real estate market is like a living, breathing entity. It ebbs and flows, influenced by numerous factors from economic conditions to interest rates, and even changing societal trends. As a real estate investor, *staying updated on market trends and conditions* is not just a good practice - it's a necessity.

If I were to count the number of times thorough market research saved my skin, we'd be here all day. Remember, every property comes with its own story and potential. The more you know about a property, its neighborhood, and the local amenities, the better equipped you'll be to make a sound investment decision.

Always remember, *your research is your compass* in this journey of real estate investing.

The real estate industry is like a vast web. It's all about connections and relationships. Trust me when I say, your network can be your most valuable asset. Attend industry events, engage with other real estate professionals, join investor associations - these are your opportunities to learn, gain insights, and even find your next big investment opportunity.

Think of it as building your very own real estate family. The family members are your guides, mentors, and partners in this exciting journey. Remember, you're not alone in this adventure.

An investment in knowledge, they say, pays the best interest. It's never been truer than in the world of real estate investing. The industry is always evolving, and the best practices of today might be obsolete tomorrow. As an investor, it's your responsibility to stay informed.

Invest in your education. Attend seminars, webinars, and training programs. Read books, listen to podcasts, and follow industry leaders. This knowledge isn't just power - it's your ticket to success in this ever-changing landscape.

Parting Words

As we conclude our journey through the realm of real estate investing with single-family properties, I want you to think of these final words as the start of a new chapter. We've traveled the winding road of investing together, picking up valuable lessons at each twist and turn. Now, it's time to put these lessons into practice and begin your own adventure.

I cannot stress enough the importance of celebrating every step of your journey, no matter how small. Our road to success is paved with both triumphs and trials, each a unique opportunity to grow. *Remember, every achievement, big or small, is a stepping stone on your path to success.*

Do you remember the first time you rode a bicycle? How you fell, dusted yourself off, and tried again, until you finally rode off into the sun? This image mirrors our adventure in real estate. We're bound to stumble, but every fall is a chance to learn.

Let me share a personal anecdote. In my earlier days, I botched a negotiation for what seemed to be a promising deal. I was disappointed, of course. However, instead of wallowing in self-pity, I analyzed my mistakes and saw them as a learning opportunity. Today, I look back at that slip-up as one of my most valuable lessons.

After celebrating and learning from your experiences, it's time to look to the future. Your journey doesn't end with one successful deal, or even several. Like a curious explorer, you should always be on the lookout for the next opportunity. *Think of your real estate journey as an unending adventure, filled with potential and ripe for exploration.*

As we draw to a close, remember that this guide is just the start of your journey. It's your springboard to success, your map to navigate the world of single-family property investing. *With these ten steps as your beacon, you're ready to embark on your journey to success.*

So, buckle up, keep your eyes on the horizon, and take the first step toward your dreams. The world of real estate investing awaits you!

If you enjoyed this book or found it helpful I'd be very grateful if you'd post a short review on Amazon ©. Your support really does make a difference. I read all the reviews personally to get your feedback and make this book even better.

End

Made in the USA
Middletown, DE
29 August 2024

59945002R00046